The Rocky Mountains

For the Hendrick family—M. D. B.

For Sophia, Leonardo, Tessa,
and Anna—J. G. W.

SIMON SPOTLIGHT
An imprint of Simon & Schuster Children's Publishing Division
1230 Avenue of the Americas, New York, NY 10020
This Simon Spotlight edition August 2019
First Aladdin Paperbacks edition October 2006
Text copyright © 2006 by Marion Dane Bauer
Illustrations copyright © 2006 by John Wallace
SIMON SPOTLIGHT, READY-TO-READ, and colophon are registered
trademarks of Simon & Schuster, Inc.
For information about special discounts for bulk purchases, please
contact Simon & Schuster Special Sales at 1-866-506-1949 or
business@simonandschuster.com.
Manufactured in the United States of America 0719 LAK
2 4 6 8 10 9 7 5 3 1
Library of Congress Cataloging-in-Publication Data
Bauer, Marion Dane.
The Rocky Mountains / by Marion Dane Bauer ;
illustrated by John Wallace.
p. cm.—(Wonders of America)
1. Rocky Mountains—Description and travel—Juvenile literature.
2. Natural history—Rocky Mountains—Juvenile literature.
I. Wallace, John, 1966– ill. II. Title. III. Series: Bauer, Marion Dane.
Wonders of America.
F721.B28 2006   917.804—dc22   2005028026
ISBN 978-1-5344-4539-0 (hc)
ISBN 978-0-689-86948-8 (pbk)

Wonders of America

The Rocky Mountains

By **Marion Dane Bauer**

Illustrated by **John Wallace**

Ready-to-Read

SIMON SPOTLIGHT
New York London Toronto Sydney New Delhi

The Rocky Mountains
form the backbone
of North America.
That backbone is more than
3,000 miles long.

The Rockies take their name from their rocky peaks.

The Rocky Mountains form North America's Continental Divide.

They divide the rivers
that flow
to the Atlantic Ocean
from those that flow
to the Pacific Ocean.

9

Coyotes

and wolves,

bison

and elk live in
the Rocky Mountains.

Mountain lions live there,

and grizzly bears do too.

So do Rocky Mountain goats

and bighorn sheep.

Ptarmigans (tar-mi-guns),
birds with feathers
on their feet,
live in the cold,
rocky peaks.

People live in
the Rockies too.
People have lived there
for the last 11,000 years.

When the first settlers
arrived from Europe,
Shoshone lived in Idaho,

Blackfeet in Montana,

and Utes in Colorado.

Now many different
people live in the
Rockies.

Others come to visit
the mountains from
all over the world.

Some come to hike

and some to ski.

Some come to climb
the mountains.

Some come just to be
part of the quiet beauty.

We are very lucky
that the Rocky Mountains
are here today.

Our country has
a beautiful backbone!

31

Interesting Facts about the Rocky Mountains

★ To be called a mountain, land must rise to 1,000 feet or more. Many of the Rocky Mountains are more than 14,000 feet tall. In Colorado alone more than 50 peaks are over 14,000 feet.

★ The Rocky Mountains formed in different ways. The earth wrinkled to make some of them. Some were made because the earth cracked. Then pressure pushed one side of the crack up. Volcanoes made some of the Rocky Mountains. They poured out hot liquid that cooled into rock. All this happened long, long ago.

★ Over a long, long time mountains can be worn down by wind and dust. They can also be worn down by sliding snow and ice. Rain wears a mountain down too.

★ The Rockies get very little rain. They do get snow, though. Most of the water that feeds the mountains and the land around them comes from melted snow.

★ Lewis and Clark were among the first white explorers to cross the Rockies. When they got to the top of the first pass, they expected to be able to ride a river down the other side all the way to the Pacific Ocean. What they saw from that pass were many, many more mountains.